Guru Stew

Linda J McLeod

BLACK COCKIE PRESS

Guru Stew

Published by Black Cockie Press

Copyright © Linda J McLeod 2019

The moral right of the author has been asserted

Cover design © Natalie Muller 2019

Distributed by IngramSpark

Printed by IngramSpark

ISBN: 9780648136675

DEDICATION

*For my dad, family and friends and my publisher,
who encouraged my ditty obsession,
giving me the confidence to serve with verse and dish up Guru Stew.*

Enjoy!

NARRATIVE VERSE

CLAN McLEOD

GEORGE THE DROVER

THE MAN FROM ISABELLA

THE BUSH WALK

A SIGHT FOR SORE EYES

THREEPENCE

GRANDDAD

POT LUCK

LAMP LADIES

HE NEVER SAID

TALL TALES

THAT SHED

REVAMPED

FUNNY

MY SECRET PASSION

THE ONE WOMAN SHOW

COMPOST

THE SIEVE

MEMOIRS

SHELVED

CLEAN OUT

STAR GAZING

A LITTLE FIBULAR

MRS BLACKWOOD

SURPRISE NIGHT

THE NEIGHBOURS

TAI CHI

KITCHEN BLUES

THE UNHOSPITABLE HOSPITAL

EEVEE

WOMEN

GURU STEW

LOVE THY NEIGHBOURS

MY DESIDERATA

TRUTH HURTS

THE LONG VERSION

MUM'S THE WORD

MOTHER LOVE

THAT DAUGHTER OF MINE

LITTLE ME

TINY TESTIMONIALS

FIFTYISH

OPPORTUNITY KNOCKS

AS TIME SLIPS BY

MY MESS

A RIDE INSIDE

HUSBANDS AND CARS

VEERING LEFT

THE HUSBAND

SOMEWHERE OVER THE RAINBOW

GOOD FRIDAY

MENS' BUSINESS

DRIVEWAY BLUES

THE PICK UP LINE

CATCH OF THE DAY

FRIENDSHIP

HAZELIZATION

WARM AND FUZZY

THE NOTE

THE BOOK KEEPER

PARENTS

THE GATHERING

MOTHER'S PEARLS

MUM'S WAY

ELEVEN / ELEVEN

VERY FUNNY DAD...

UP THERE

SPIRITUAL

THANK YOU

THE THISTLE

SHOAL

SAINT MARY of the CROSS MacKILLOP

ETERNAL

LINDA'S ISLAND

TO BE STILL

HOLD FAST

DREAM STREAM

CALLIOPSIS

BE ALIVE

NARRATIVE VERSE

CLAN McLEOD

Anne and Alexander set sail for New South Wales
on a voyage of discovery they weathered storms and gales.
In eighteen hundred and thirty five Saint George sailed into Port,
to Sydney town Australia their hopes and dreams were brought.

From Hebrides to colonies they had to readjust
survival in this southern land made family a must.
Anne and Alexander learnt to live and love this land
they made a home away from home always hand in hand.

They settled down on Brownlow Hill and bought some seeds to sow,
they also planted orchards and watched their garden grow.
To make a living off the land was the family's' plan,
a tenant farm, the very first, successfully they ran.

Farming was essential, they had to feed their flock
eleven bonny children all of Scottish stock.
They lived the family motto to Hold Fast come what may
they all held fast together to face what came their way.

Craftsmen, teachers, poets I hope we've done them proud
we are a mighty family, we are the clan McLeod.
We went back to Brownlow Hill to celebrate our roots,
we are Anne and Alexander's Australian flavoured fruits.

GEORGE THE DROVER

In his head he was a drover...
In reality a driver,
a chauffeur and mechanic
George Honey the survivor.

Returning home from war
George had safely come,
he married Edith Greenfield
and soon they had a son.

Hard times meant his skills
were all to no avail,
he dreamt of going droving
so the three of them set sail.

Australia welcomed immigrants
£10.00 Pomms from Kent,
the lady and the gentleman
to Sydney's North they went.

A tiny town called Brookvale
held homeland memories..
picnics on the fresh, green grass
'neath shady willow trees.

Nellie, Stan and Archie
lived in the neighbourhood,

life here in Australia
was looking pretty good!

A daughter for the Honeys'
a baby born so sweet,
an addition to the family
made their hive complete.

Selling eggs and chook poo
may seem a bit ho-hum,
they always saw the sunny side
to keep from feeling glum.

George dreamt he was a-droving
as the chooks he mustered,
he loved his comfy home
and Edith's pies and custard.

THE MAN FROM ISABELLA

The sketch sits on the mantelpiece in its old wooden frame
it tells a gruesome story which in time has gathered fame,
a conversation starter, it's a yarn, but it's the truth
a tribute to young Bob and the boldness of his youth.

Dated nineteen twenty two by Mr F Mahoney,
he was a true blue mate of Bob, so we know it isn't phoney.
Now Frankie was real talented, at capturing the day
sketching the events in black and white and grey.

The Stapletons were graziers and foxes raided stock,
so they had organized a hunt to protect their precious flock.
They gathered down at Woodford farm, the day unusually warm,
Granddad Robert Stapleton, Frank, Mel, Syd and Norm.

They'd gone to Isabella, as was their monthly habit,
with visions of the hunting spree, they could almost taste the rabbit.
The neighbours too joined in the shoot, that is the country way,
everyone took part in a most successful day.

The day was drawing to a close, the dogs had run ahead
racing off back home where they would soon be fed.

While the men shared out the spoils they heard blood curdling sounds
could it be these mournful cries came out of their greyhounds?

They raced toward the place where the howling dogs had been
but they had never seen the likes of this devastating scene,
scattered all around was hair and blood and guts
the bloodied, dead remains of Grandad's favourite mutts.

Standing there before them was the cunning, vicious beast
he must have stood ten foot tall at the very, very least.
The picture shows a running man wielding forth a club
as he chased the mighty giant back into the scrub.

He's pictured here for all to see his brave and gallant charge
against the creature from the bush, strong and fierce and large.
I've tried my best to relate just what the artist drew
the day young Bob Stapleton met the killer kangaroo.

THE BUSH WALK

We walked without a care out in the fresh Blue Mountain air,
a freedom that we never, ever knew.
We descended by the Furber, but it was still much further
till the landslide came within our view.

Well we three mates were talkin' and quite unaware of walkin'
not lookin' at the path ahead but up into the sky.
Pretty soon we all were wishin' we'd kept tabs on our position
when somethin' over yonder caught our eye.

There was writin' on a sign all about the old coal mine
it said the way was DANGEROUS !
But though there was no doubt it meant you really should keep out,
we reckoned that this surely wasn't us.

We knew we really shouldn't but no one said we couldn't
so we explored the old forgotten track,
but after our adventure, like an act of mad dementia
we couldn't seem to find the right way back.

We hadn't gone on long 'till we figured somethin's wrong…
the wretched path had lead us far astray,
so though we never meant to… the direction that we went to
was heading up Mount Solitary way.

Our recklessness had cost us an' our rashness now had lost us
we only had ourselves to blame

Guru Stew 15

'cause we'd not be in this crap if we were following a map
and paid attention to the signs that came.

Even then we didn't stop, we kept on goin' to the top
we figured we might find our bearin's there.
The view from way up there had made us gawk and stare
to see the beauty and the terror everywhere.

The view from there was fine, we didn't see the lookout sign,
warning DANGER! WATCH THE EDGE!
'twas then our vision splendid most abruptly came and ended
as we went walking off that very ledge.

Well we three mates then fell; it was like goin' down to hell
we fell and met our fate that sorry day.
Then we saw a neon sign, with its origins Divine
so we followed it and now we know the way.

A SIGHT FOR SORE EYES

'twas just after Christmas, the New year was nigh,
when backpackers swarmed the Blue Mountains high.
The weather was warm, not at all cold
now listen to how events did unfold.

'twas late in the arvo when they all came out
the short and the tall, the slim and the stout.
Visions of tourists had danced in our heads
but we'd never dreamt they'd be wearing no threads!

Away to the lookout we flew and we dashed,
it's not every day sight seers are flashed.
The light on the breasts of those down below
gave the lustre of midday to the innocent show.

When what to our wondering eyes should appear...
but the miniature tourists who'd got off their gear.
Their prancing and squealing meant they never knew
that we were all there admiring the view.

To the call of the wild they'd come with no fear
to bathe in the beauty of nature right here.
They'd come to be free in our water falls,
all private and shady with iron stone walls.

A photographer happened to be there that day
as the foreigners put on their public display,

and soon he had sent around the whole globe
pictures of tourist who chose to disrobe.

Seeing as tourism is our main aim
we'll try to accommodate those without shame,
new signs we'll erect
"take care and don't slip and wear plenty of sunscreen, when you skinny dip."

THREEPENCE

There was no movement at the station
for the train had come and gone
so I waited for the next to come along.
While I sat awaiting and was looking all around
I found a long lost threepence half buried in the ground.
A story true and wondrous was what the three pence told
and the wisdom it had gleaned more valuable than gold.

"I started out all shiny, minted nineteen thirty three,
excited by the prospect of all that I would see.
I aimed to serve my country, although I'm only small
I played my part, I did my bit, I gave to them my all.

I've had a taste of puddings, both magical and plain.
I've been a bet for a cigarette and then won back again.
I've travelled far in pockets, along with shopping dockets,
I've passed through many, many hands.

For a load of seed first grade I'm what the farmer paid
and the profit a washer woman made.
Once I was a bribe, 'till I was put inside
a slot and bought a ticket to a show.

I've been begged, borrowed, stolen, lost and found,
I've kept company with Shillings and with Pounds,
but to one who hasn't any, not even half a penny,
I was the answer to a prayer.

I felt my worth decreasing as the years went on and on,
I remember being valued back when I first shone.
I've played a good sound innings since back at my beginnings,
I've done my Three penny bit."

Now a shade of melancholy came over the whole speech
and I recognized a lesson, a momentary blessin'
had been put within my reach.
The coin became redundant, superseded by the cent
and has laid here ever since, embattled, worn and spent.

GRANDDAD

Our Granddad was a bloke who loved to share a joke;
we hung on every single word he said.
His stature was immense, his character intense,
he was Blue Mountain stock, both born and bred.

We're family and we're friends, on each other we depend
so we'd come to see our Granddad we adored,
but we found he looked so frail, his face was deathly pale,
yet just being there we felt more reassured.

Our Granddad, good and wise, sometimes told white lies
in telling them he wouldn't even blink.
Yes he loved to spin a yarn, inside a shed or barn,
he'd finish with a cheeky nod and wink.

He'd often pluck a tale, with elaborate detail
embellishing the highlights of his youth,
then he would entertain, repeating it again
even though it was without a grain of truth.

*

In his wild erratic state some visions came of late
of all he'd seen and done and where and why...
So mustering his strength, he told us all at length;
revisiting his grand old days gone by.

The family bond is true, we see each other through
so we'd come to say farewell and pay respects.

As the crowd all gave a cheer, he grinned from ear to ear,
we knew this was a man with few regrets.

His talk that night was loose, though served another use
diverting the attention from his plight.
As we gathered round and listened, eyes all fairly glistened
as he passed towards the Everlasting Light.

POT LUCK

The pot sat on the doorstep
in a sad and sorry state.
At night it cried "Woe is me,
look what's become my fate."

A storm came over the mountain,
it threatened overhead.
The house was in the firing line,
our hearts were full of dread.

The dye was cast for a mighty blast,
on a mission it had come.
The rain poured down from darkened skies
pounding like a drum.

We saw the lightning strike close by,
we heard the fearful sound
as exploding agapanthus
hurtled to the ground.

All disembowelled, the old pot howled
it held itself in fright;
a blessing in disguise
by a shard of deadly light.

"Muller's luck, I've been struck,
at last I have been freed.

Never again will I be filled
with tubas, dirt and weed!"

We knew then, at ten past ten,
the family curse was broken!
But non- believing sceptics say...
we're crazy or we're jokin'.

LAMP LADIES

They are so beautiful, elegant, styled in Art Nouveau,
innocent erotica though you may never know.

Like toys in nursery land his statues will awake
and take him on a fantasy to make a grown man quake.

Standing up in readiness their fans alight, on fire,
coming in his dreams fulfilling his desire.

His fantasy is so strong, experience can't surpass
the excitement when he feels their fans tickling his arse.

He offers no resistance, he's in no state to fight
he willingly succumbs to his Ladies of the Night.

HE NEVER SAID

Dave said he would be working at the Carrington hotel...
I didn't catch his meaning but presumed that he would tell...
but he was called away before it all was said,
so as he'd peaked my interest I imagined it instead!

Was he working as a waiter, a barman or a bouncer,
a piano playing maestro or a D.J type announcer?
I pondered what he meant when he said he would be "working",
did he mean he'd bare it all?? He's never one for shirking!!

Images formed in my head as I began to wonder...
My goodness no, let it go, this could be a monumental blunder.
I'm always taking hold of the wrong end of the stick,
it seems I'm just too gullible and he doesn't miss a trick.

He pulled my leg some more, he winked and he was smirking;
Yes he had been working hard and yes he had been jerking,
he'd been standing, squatting, crouching, and laying,
rubbing, smoothing, screwing, aligning and displaying.

Now Dave was paid in "mates rates" so I'm not completely wrong;
he'd been working like a navvy and he'd been working for a song.
And when it all came out it was just as I suspected
the shelving on the office wall was all that he'd erected.

TALL TALES

Dave always has a tale to tell
though some of it's just noise,
he likes to chew the fat
and go on yarning with the boys.
He lives and breathes the mountains,
he's known to mountain folk
as a larrikin, a scallywag,
an all round Aussie bloke.
To and from his Hartley home
he drove the western road
he knew each nasty bend
and his driving prowess showed.
We know he tells tall tales
and so there's no mistakes
I'll tell you just what happened
the night Dave lost his brakes.
The night he felt the brakes let go
in his beloved Ute
he reckoned he could get her home
by their usual route.
The failure of the master meant
he'd have to ride the clutch,
he drew on all his expertise
and used his skilful touch.
He drove on up to Blackheath,
he didn't have much choice,

he followed The Great Western
'till he came to old Mount Boyce.
Soon he'd reached Mount Vic Pass
with hairy bends ahead
the road from here wound all downhill,
his heart was full of dread.
He said his prayers, he swallowed hard,
his head and heart both pounded,
he held his nerve, he grit his teeth
as twists and turns he rounded.
Descending now was quick and steep
he slipped her in low gear
and like the Snowy River Man
our hero showed no fear!
The highway it was clear right through,
he thanked his lucky stars
he'd met with no mishap
no kangaroos or cars.
That night when he was safely home
in the arms of his darling wife
he told her of his tedious day...
and then the ride of his life.

THAT SHED

That shed it still holds secrets hid within its walls
of times well spent together, that shed of distant calls.
Fifty years of memories are kept inside that shed
some are scattered all around, some are cased in lead.

Flying high like bunting, flagging black and white and red
I'm filled with mixed emotions when I go in that shed.
Fishing rods and gold pans cast a sentimental spell
finding memories of good times
when all that was, was well.
My father's tools and gadgets on the benches still do lay,
projects he had started, to finish another day.

That shed's a precious treasure trove, Aladdin's secret cave
that I can loot and plunder or else I can just save,
guard, defend and nurture as a space to call my own,
a place of childhood fancies and the attachments it has grown.
A place of self-recovery is where I'm often led,
a watershed discovery deep inside that shed.

REVAMPED

She's stood out there for eighty years,
she's part of history's page,
she's having work that's overdue
'cause she looks and feels her age.

She's under reconstruction
so he's sparing no expense
he's made a list of things he'll need
and used wire from the fence.

He's bought a bag of best cement
to hold the old, old bricks
and cut saplings for the beams
in the wall he plans to fix.

He's purchased brand new roofing screws
for they'd gone without a trace
and even found some guttering
lying 'round the place.

Steel sheet and corrugate
not quite rusted through
don't need to be replaced yet
the old will have to do.

Two glass doors came his way
much to his surprise,

they are the icing on the cake
to complete his enterprise.

We'll have a grand shed warming
so the neighbours all can see
the fruit of all his labours
and the parts he found for free.

FUNNY

Guru Stew 32

MY SECRET PASSION

A few moments of fun is all that I need
to tickle my fancy! but where will it lead?...

I like to indulge, I like to expand,
but where will it lead? will it get out of hand?

I do it in daylight, I do it at night,
I over indulge though I know it's not right.

I do it alone, or in a crowd,
I do it in silence, I do it out loud.

I do it in gardens and under the trees,
I do it when and where ever I please.

I do it at home, at work and when shopping,
I'm out of control, there's no cure or stopping.

I do it on tables, I do it in bed,
see where my common compulsion has led.

I do it in Spring, Summer, Autumn and Winter
with or without my laptop and printer.

THE ONE WOMAN SHOW

She looks so neat and nice, she's always so well groomed
and quiet as a mouse, or so everyone assumed.
This woman was a poet, irreverent and improper
her friends were all aghast at this but too polite to stop her.

She didn't have an inkling of what was right or wrong
if she'd entered in a talent show they'd have given her the gong!
Her funnies weren't so funny, I'm afraid she looked a fool
but she didn't take the hint and was as stubborn as a mule.

She couldn't see the audience from where she stood on stage
she couldn't see their faces so 'twas difficult to gauge
whether they were interested or had they gone to sleep??
and because she'd gone stone deaf she couldn't hear a peep.

She couldn't hear her intro so she always missed her cue,
she couldn't hear their heckles, she couldn't hear them "BOO."
I don't want to offend her so please don't tell her what I said
the truth is that her "talent" was concocted in her head.

COMPOST

Decomposing matter is filling up my head
of things that happened yesterday
of what was heard and said.
Like organic compost it makes my garden thrive,
when I sow in fertile ground the seeds will come alive.
Piling up and breaking down of all the information
promotes ideas to root and flourish finding animation.
Poetry and garden critics will say I've lost the plot
that what I count as nourishment to them it is just rot.

THE SIEVE

I forget, forget, forget, I forget what I forgot
my family's not surprised I do it such a lot.
The voice inside me said, "You need to order gas."
By the time I reached the phone I'd forgotten it alas.
Cold showers for a week surely should remind
not to re offend with another of this kind.
In my little car I've had a few close shaves
but luckily for me I've had as many saves.
I forgot the handbrake when parking on a slope,
I had to get a tow truck to winch it on a rope.
I misplaced twenty dollars, I searched the whole house through,
did it slip out of my pocket and float on down the loo?
One day I lost my wedding ring, 'twas hidden out of sight
I forgot when I last saw it, it gave me such a fright.
My day to day adventures occupy and make
for an interesting life as I await my next mistake.

MEMOIRS

In years to come when memory fades,
when I am old and grey
I'll have a rhyming record
of every special day.

Mind you that time's approaching,
I need triggers, clues and prompts,
my memory's not too clear
it forgets and often wants.

Here's my way of scrap booking
I use words instead of pictures
I frame the scenes in poetry
instead of fancy fixtures.

I try to memorize my rhymes,
I write them in a book,
I just hope that I can find it
should I ever need to look.

Some people call it twaddle,
it's because they cannot see
the power of the words that rhyme
and how they work for me.

SHELVED

I know that there is not much hope
into the depths I feel and grope
longing for the things long spent
wondering where my memory went.

My patience now is wearing thin
as I see the spot I'm in,
wedged between the past and present
my dilemma is not pleasant.

Some people have such great recall
of details large and details small
my recollection is quite hazy
sometimes I think I'm going crazy.

Digging deeper, feel and probe
into the depths of my wardrobe
it isn't what it used to be
look what has become of me.

CLEAN OUT

The time has come I have to say
I've lots of stuff to throw away.
But as you know one must go through
deciding where and what to do
with each and every treasure.
"Does it still invoke some pleasure?"
Is the question you must ask,
as you set about this task.
There's all the things you kept "In case..."
but thought were lost without a trace,
now's the time to throw them out...
Be ruthless! But if you're in doubt...?
and erring on the side of caution
decide to stow away a portion
when you next come to inspect it
you'll wonder why on earth you kept it!

STAR GAZING

Two dull life forms stood out there
looking skyward, wondering where
and why and how and what...
was this natural or was it not?
Phenomena so rarely seen
here and now, what did it mean?
Recalling theories learnt in college
between the two they shared their knowledge.
They boldly went where no man's gone,
but they got it completely wrong.
The cause of such a great commotion...
Spotlights for a film promotion!

A LITTLE FIBULAR

You wanted to know how I met the floor,
over what did I trip and is it still sore?
Here is what happened, when I broke my fib,
here is my version, with a bit of add lib.

I was practising cartwheels for my gymnastic routine
rolling and tumbling with twists in between,
then my attention I gave to the rings
with all of the focus this discipline brings,
into my vaulting I next hurled myself
light as the air, like a fairy or elf.

When I had finished my routine was slick
so I hurried inside, but I hurried too quick,
for one who is nimble, balanced and sure
it's hard to believe that I hit the floor.
I don't like to admit I fell over my feet
it may harm my chance of an Olympian seat.

MRS BLACKWOOD

Now that she is getting on
she's showing too much cleavage,
it's because of her treemendous size,
causing such great heavage.

It's only when you near her
you see she's lost her youthful look,
she no longer wears an air of grace...
on the whole she's looking pretty crook.

And then on close inspection
she bears deep, savage scars,
from her many irritations
inflicted by galahs.

She's heading for a break down,
and it isn't IF, but WHEN?
She isn't what she used to be...
she no longer rates a TEN!

Her integrity is compromised
one day her sides will split
but if she falls down on the chook house
we'll all be in the shit!

SURPRISE NIGHT

It was not your average party night
but it was certain to delight,
Tupperware just can't compete
with a fine Egyptian sheet.

The quality was quite exotic,
soft and smooth a touch erotic.
As the threads were being counted
our expectations now were mounted.

There were oohs, aahs, growls and howls
when we saw the big thick towels.
The climax was the low, low price
which made the sale twice as nice.

My poor sheets are really thinin'
so I indulged in new bed linen.
I'm sure my hubby won't protest;
between the sheets he likes best!

THE NEIGHBOURS

New neighbours 'ave moved in
yonder down the street
in the place the other side of
the one that's kept so neat.

Y' know the yard where the fence is broke
the one with giant trees,
the garden's over grown
an' the grass is over y'r knees?

The place is so run-down
per'aps they'll renovate
they'd better soon get started
before it is too late.

If they've come down from up north
I'll bet they're feeling cold,
they won't 'ave modern cons
the place is too darn old.

They may 'ave come 'ere from the bush
an' want to settle 'ere
or per'aps they are just passing through
'till they are in the clear.

Well this new lot 'ave moved in,
we'll 'ave to wait an' see

if they are the family type
an' 'ow many there will be.

Will they be good neighbours?
This 'll be the test...
will they 'ave young magpies
falling from their nest.

TAI CHI

I'm learning the way of an ancient art
I've joined a class and I'm taking part,
the first week that I went along
I tried so hard but got it wrong.

Our teacher moved with poise and grace
demonstrating steps and pace.
Renatta said we'd all soon get it
but too soon I did forget it.

Still my body would not copy
legs won't move, arms too sloppy.
Then in my head I made the decision
to master the art with great precision.

Practice, practice, practice more,
moving slowly, smooth and sure.
I'll practice morning, noon and night
'till I get my Tai chi right.

KITCHEN BLUES

I'm having red hot flushes,
it's hot here in the kitchen,
I'm picking up bad vibes
from all the nasty friction.

I much prefer a quiet life
without the melodramas,
I'm feeling rather fragile
so I'll stay in my pyjamas.

I'll go on strike, I'll work from home
writing ditties and non-fiction
about the endless goings on
in this circus of a kitchen.

I could write a great soap opera
with what I've heard and seen,
they'd perform it in the theatres
and on the silver screen.

And so I'll say again,
I'll stand by my conviction
that we would all be better off
without the kitchen bitch'n'!

THE UNHOSPITABLE HOSPITAL

Here's a tale of daring do of which you've never heard
it isn't common knowledge so you mustn't say a word...
This bloke who was a no good, a scoundrel and a pest
came to the Blue Mountains from all the way out west.

He snuck into our hospital to find a place to hide
but then he lost his bearings once he was inside.
He didn't heed the warning signs Greg placed along the hall
the floor was wet and slippery, but he managed not to fall.

He found a place to catch his breath behind an open door
and there he stayed all quiet till absolutely sure...
security were off his back so he could make his break,
but which way was the exit? Which way should he take?

He didn't see them coming as they approached the turn
all loaded up with biscuits, milk, coffee and tea urn.
The exit signs confused him, where was Woodlands Road?
He asked the nice tea ladies, Mary pointed as she showed...

'twas then old Ned came running, he gave a warning shout
so Linda steered her tea trolley to cut off the way out.
Lois with her cleaning kit and Gary's garbage cart
blocked the other exit and together did their part.

They took the villain out of here and put him into gaol,
but the last thing that I heard is now he's out on bail.

Guru Stew 48

I've told you of the drama that unfolded last weekend
you can be the judge, if it's true or just pretend!

EEVEE

On the roof I heard rain pouring,
at the door the cat was pawing.
Cat went out into the rain
but promised to come back again.
Cats and dogs were raining down
I feared that pussy cat might drown.
Wet and cold and white with fright
cat endured the stormy night.
Cat came home late next day
regretting having gone away.
Now in will stay our pussykins
at least 'till she has sprouted fins.

WOMEN

GURU STEW

We're all part of guru stew
bits of me and bits of you
our pot full of resources
makes for rich and varied sauces
nourishment to eat
the veggies and the meat
each mouthful is unique
with its flavour and mystique
it satisfies and purifies
here the mystery lies...
the recipe is handed on
keep it rich keep it strong
it is our very womanhood
which makes us taste so very good.

LOVE THY NEIGHBOURS

Moving on is what they call it,
we come, we meet, we stay...
cup of sugar, babysit,
I'll miss you when you go away.

Women share each other's burdens
to lighten up their days,
advice and understanding
are two of women's ways.

A bit of give, a bit of take
is how we help each other.
It's happened since the dawn of time
we are sisters, we are mothers.

Even when we say farewell
history repeats.
A friend in need is a friend indeed
the communal heart still beats.

The comings and the goings
as the years unfold
attest to female fellowship
friends with hearts of gold.

MY DESIDERATA

If the hat fits wear it.
Don't fight it or you'll tear it.

Be at home with all that's you,
some things old, some things new.

Welcome in new ideas,
casting out doubts and fears.

Even hardship has its place,
remember that it's not a race.

As life goes, it ebbs and flows,
just to keep you on your toes.

Your family needs someone steady,
someone who is always ready.

But let them know you need your space,
time to fill with inner grace.

Affirmations positive
give you nourishment to live.

It's exciting biting zest.
Wear the hat that fits you best!

TRUTH HURTS

I looked in the mirror
when specs I was trying
From what I saw next
I knew I'd been lying.
The reflection I saw
was so very clear
I wished I'd not gone
so close and so near
The dust on the mirror
and my weak eyes
had suggested to me
a different disguise.
I had the impression
I wasn't too bad
now facing the facts
I admit I'm quite sad.
The damage is done,
there's no turning back,
the skin on my face
is all wrinkled and slack.
Remember my lovelies
that I see through
rose coloured glasses
when looking at you!

THE LONG VERSION

Oh Mum you're so frustrating
the way you seem to find
some piece of information
you've been storing in your mind.
You often have a tale to tell,
or an article to show,
some obscure connection
a picture or photo.
You go off on a tangent
of who and why and when
you eventually come back
to where you were again.
We stare at our dear Mother
saying "look where this has led."
only now we're much the wiser
having heard what she has said!

MUM'S THE WORD

I'm the mother of two daughters
I'm torn between the pair,
sometimes it is quite difficult
when they both want their share.

I try to be supportive
while sitting on the fence,
I try to give a balanced view
though the challenge is immense.

I'm leader of the peace talks,
I am the go between,
I try to put the fire out
before there is a scene.

Though they fight like cat and dog
it really all depends...
for when they can see eye to eye
they are the best of friends.

How to satisfy them both
is the answer to the riddle,
but 'till the day they can agree
I'm piggy in the middle.

MOTHER LOVE

I'm chauffeur, chef and washer woman
in a large hotel
I'm over worked and under paid
by the clientele.

They say they let me do it
because I do it best,
they say they let me do it
lest I suffer empty nest.

Even when it irks me
and inside it makes me rile
I keep on being Mother
giving service with a smile.

But I do get board and lodging
so I s'ppose I can't complain
"Oh Mother dear come here, come here
can you get out this stain?"

THAT DAUGHTER OF MINE

I try not to be a naggy old hag,
but at times I just have to say,

"Hang up your dress, your room is a mess,
And it's your turn to clean the cat tray."

I try to imbue a sense of can do,
to encourage, empower and move,
to give wisdom to see how it would be
if she would get out of her groove.

"Too busy today, can't help the delay,
I'll do it tomorrow for sure."

I won't hold my breath, she'll be my death,
I'll believe it when I can see floor.

LITTLE ME

I am a Lindavidual,
I'm gifted with a curse
from time to time I slip into rhyme
my mind goes in reverse.
My family find me frustrating
but they shouldn't as at least
it keeps me ever occupied
and they'd miss it if I ceased.

TINY TESTIMONIALS

How can one not be sentimental
for baby things, hair and dental
wrapped up in a little box
along with tiny baby socks.

FIFTYISH

As I approach my fiftieth year
let me state and make it clear
I won't go down without a fight
I'll face the foe with all my might.
I won't succumb to moods of gloom,
for that I haven't any room
I'll not put away my passions
or wear old lady, frumpy fashions
and if I want I'll go sky diving
or even take up rally driving.
Fifty is a little hurdle
it doesn't mean I need a girdle
or such things to remind
my youth and bum are far behind,
my shapely parts and saggy arms
are among my feminine charms,
I've got more now than I had
but I'm told this isn't bad.
Fifty's full of mixed emotions,
Ointments, balms, creams and lotions
to rejuvenate the skin I'm in
damaged, wrinkled, spotty, thin.
I may need aids for eyes and ears
but so do many of my peers,
my muscles and my memory waning
both could do with some retraining.
I now look like my mum did

when I was a teenage kid
but then I didn't understand
Fifty isn't bland...it's GRAND!

OPPORTUNITY KNOCKS

"A golden opportunity in this your fiftieth year..."
I don't know what it is yet
as I did not hear too clear.

Often what I hear
doesn't make much sense
the clues are far too subtle
for pity sake I'm dense.

Too frequently it seems
I get the wrong end of the stick
I end up in trouble
my wit is not so quick.

I'm oblivious to obvious
I'm stumbling in the dark
I have to make a note
of where on earth I park.

Something great, momentous
awaits me down the line
but I may not recognize it
without a neon sign.

Guru Stew 64

AS TIME SLIPS BY

My name is Linda Josephine, born nineteen fifty eight.
I slipped into my family: Mum, Dad, Jude and Cate.

I slipped in and out of childhood without too much of a fuss,
Family life was focused on me and we and us.

High school grades were sliding, I was not a switched on student
leaving at a tender age was thought to be most prudent.

Working girl, fashion plate, slipping into gear,
being independent while keeping family near.

Married in the seventies, I was just a slip of a bride,
still in my teenage years but my eyes were open wide.

Sister, daughter, mother, wife.
The stage was set for the rest of my life.

Slip and slide, babies cried, housework left undone.
Balancing priorities, learning on the run.

Sweet and sour, bloom and flower, my thirties really slid,
cleaner, chef and washer woman, looking after kids.

Forties were a bit ho hum, I slipped back into work,
the pace of daily routines simply went berserk.

The fifties slide went side by side family, work and play.
A challenge to my stamina every single day.

Been there, done that, love and understanding.
Granma now, I have know-how but life is less demanding.

I'm slipping into something more comfortable somehow
The liberating sixties is where I'm heading now.

If life has been a slippery slide it's also been great fun
I have a funny feeling life has just begun!

MY MESS

You know how it is when you're stuck in a rut,
the nothingness feeling gnawing your gut
and negative vibes pervade every joint
the question you ask is "What is the point?"

"Does anyone out there know what I mean?"
You feel all alone, or so it would seem,
all that you do is cook, wash and clean,
"Isn't there more?" you hear yourself scream.

The answer is yes, you already know,
search for the answer deep down below.
Look under the surface, like dusting a shelf,
and soon you'll uncover more of yourself.

I clean up my act, I begin from within,
I pull up the blinds and let the sun in.
I wash away smears caused by my tears,
I sweep away cobwebs which harboured my fears.

My housework is done, for now any way,
now I am able to rest and to play.
Now that I know what causes distress
I am more careful to lessen my mess!

A RIDE INSIDE

I go back down the track I have a ticket for the train
remembering my childhood and I am there again.

Each station is a milestone on which to ruminate
the rights of adult passage to recall and contemplate.

Time has come and time's gone by from the mountains to the ocean
I've seen the sights, I've been back there on my train of dream like motion.

HUSBANDS AND CARS

VEERING LEFT

The mechanic shook his head and said
"The bad news is she's nearly dead."
"Her looks and charm are quickly fadin',
see if you can get a trade in."

Now I knew my girl was old and grey,
but I didn't want to end this way.

I remember when we used to park
by the river, in the dark,
away from others prying eyes
under clear and starry skies.

I knew my girl was old and grey
but I didn't want to end this way.

She loved to be in the great outdoors
she pulled her weight with all the chores
She carried all the camp regalia
on our trips around Australia.

I knew my girl was old and grey
but I didn't want to end this way.

I decided then to do what's best
over the cliff to her final rest.
We had come to the end of an era
I waved goodbye to my car Vera.

Guru Stew 70

THE HUSBAND

He wants to be immortalized
his daring deeds recognized
and to the world his name declare
(all be it with a poets flair.)

Off to work he does go
on weekends there's grass to mow
when it's cold he cuts the wood
he loves his wife as a husband should
he fixes everything that's broke
he doesn't drink and he doesn't smoke
he's father to our three offspring
he's generous in his offering.
His feats may not seem extraordinary
but neither are they so so ordinary.

Now may I say in my defence
he's too intense and too immense,
he's off the gauge,
to ever fit him on this page.

SOMEWHERE OVER THE RAINBOW

When we go on holiday
we make uncharted stops
searching for that model car
he checks out all the shops.

As he is approaching
his eyes light up with glee,
he can't wait to get inside
to see what he can see.

He comes out empty handed
his disappointment shows
but he vows to try again
at another place he knows.

As for me I tag along
I give a little sigh...
while he still has breath to live
his passion will not die!

GOOD FRIDAY

The explosion of the barrow wheel
meant his weekend plans were dashed
when into his Teutonic brain
a solution soon was flashed.

I could see the cogs were turning
inside his head that day,
I'd seen that look before
when problems came his way.

A wooden wheel would do the trick
although it would be slow,
he'd mend his trusty barrow
and make the bastard go!

Armed with spade and barrow
like a knight with shield and sword
he went right into battle
and his driveway he restored.

MENS' BUSINESS

He'll have all that he desires for the time when he retires
jeans and boots and socks in a stockpile 'neath the bed.
He's collecting things he may use, like wire for a broken fuse
and tools and bits and pieces stored inside the shed.

He says I shouldn't scoff, that it's not all that far off
and he's covering himself for a future rainy day,
he sees his piles growing and his face is fairly glowing
he says that this will be the only way.

His piles are so large he'll soon need a new garage
for his extra bits and pieces and his dreams,
he knows it's rather rash just to keep his secret stash
but the house and shed are busting at the seams.

He has a model car collection laid out for his inspection
he finds a new one almost every other week.
I s'pose I mustn't mention that when we're on the pension
he'll have to curb his spending so to speak.

He gambled and he dared, he was right to be prepared
and he has the feeling of security it brings.
He'll see his vision splendid, when his working days have ended
for he'll have saved up all those really useful things.

DRIVEWAY BLUES

I met him in the driveway
where he should not have been,
I met him on the corner
where we could not be seen.

Our accidental meeting
that occurred on Saturday
would surely not have happened
if he had stayed away.

A scratch upon my bumper bar
is all I have to show
but when we both collided
his car wouldn't go.

I wish I never met him
coming 'round the bend
then four hundred dollars
I wouldn't have to spend.

THE PICK UP LINE

I wandered lonely as a McLeod
that floats on high o'er vale and hill...
when all at once I saw this guy,
he stopped his car and he said Hi!

I told my mum she said "Be wary,
he may turn out to be scary."
Next day I got into his car
we drove away, we went too far.

I'm not lonely as a Muller
Tony fills my life with colour.
Now we're in our autumn days
remembering when we had no greys.

CATCH OF THE DAY

A young man out on the hunt
in his Zephyr exuding with grunt
picked up this girl
and gave her a whirl
what a risk, what a punt, what a stunt!

Their union as Mr and Mrs
was sealed with loving and kisses
in every way
they make sure they say
I'm here to grant all your wishes!

Married forty ruby years,
he's the envy of all of his peers,
for his little wife
was the catch of his life,
she was one of his better ideas!

FRIENDSHIP

HAZELIZATION

Hazeling along you go
just Hazeling along,
you always take me with you
singing your sweet song.

You sing in key, you are in tune,
you know the lyrics to the song,
you share your care with Hazel flair,
your voice is true and strong.

You show me how to keep in step
to the rhythm of the drum,
to find the beat that's right for me
you make my heart strings strum.

You harmonize and Hazelize,
a friend who brings good cheer.
I feel Hazeling sensations
when ever you are near.

Learning how to sing and dance
together is such fun.
You're my one and only,
singing, dancing
Hazelizing chum !

WARM AND FUZZY

We met way back in '85
firm friends for many years
and in that time we've sung our song
and journeyed where life steers.

It's said that when we give
we also do receive.
There is no doubt, it is the truth,
I've tried it and believe.

For when I phone or visit you
you throw it back on me;
you always are the comforter
and I the comfortee.

Guru Stew 80

THE NOTE

Over to your house for a quick break
an hour together for sanity's sake,
time for a rest, a pause in routine,
visiting Hazel changes the scene.
I put on my lippy, I put on my coat,
I put the cat out and leave them a note.
I write on the note so they know where I'm at
"Gone over to Hazel's for one of our chats."

THE BOOK KEEPER

When Noah built his arch
and the bees they made their hive
t'was the best way that they knew
to keep the breed alive.

And so our precious memories,
if they are to survive,
are kept for future reference
in Hazel's life archive.

Anyone who cares to pause
and venture to this place
will find that someone cared enough...
this woman filled with Grace.

To document our daily dos
has been her life's ambition
it's been a gift of love,
with every new addition.

The sharing of the memories
brings its own reward,
a loving testimonial
to our ever Living Lord.

Guru Stew 82

PARENTS

THE GATHERING

Catherine had counted each napkin and plate
and sent out the invites so we'd not be late.
Judy and Rod made ready the venue
presenting the feast according to menu.

The men and the boys played at their cricket
bowling and batting and taking a wicket.
Adam and Josh both baby sat,
while brothers spent time just chewing the fat.

Natalie met her cousins all new
I introduced each niece and nephew.
Tony and Rod and Michael did bring
their wives and their children and all of their things.

Brendan and Jade and family came in
they were all welcomed as part of our kin.
Helen and Laurel likewise the same
Mrs. McLeod they share as their name.

Alison, Laura and Lewis so quiet,
Reefy makes up by causing a riot!
Loretta and Bonnie a delight to behold,
none of the family left out in the cold.

Rosemary danced the arvo away,
we watched as she shook and made her hips sway.

The cameras were out to cover events,
to capture and keep the precious moments .

I recited my poem as I had prepared,
I wasn't too anxious, nervous or scared.
My mother, she knew just what I meant
when I delivered my ditty present.

Mother, so lovely, the great matriarch,
her happiness showed that we'd met the mark!
As one of the many I think I can say
we had a great time on Mum's special day.

MOTHER'S PEARLS

We were born five different girls
together strung like unique pearls.
Sisters, daughters, mothers, wives,
each involved in our own lives.

Wear and tear, the string has frayed
over time our hair has grayed,
the thread is now no longer new
yet we know that it will do.

Reconnecting makes us stronger
we'll hang on a little longer,
though far apart we keep it tight
in our way it feels just right.

Five more daughters, cousins, nieces
are threaded with the first five pieces
renewing us and making whole;
body, mind, heart and soul.

To each other hold and grasp,
Mum's the diamond studded clasp,
she's the mother of the pearls
caring for her precious girls.

Guru Stew 86

MUM'S WAY

I follow your old recipes
I've stuck them in a book
so whenever I may need them
I only have to look.

I follow your example Mum
you've helped me such a lot
with all the daily chores
and this and that what not.

I follow your advice Mum
it's been tested and it's true,
weighing up the pros and cons
'till I know just what to do.

I follow in your footsteps Mum
even though they're large and deep,
you tell me I can do it
as I take a flying leap.

I follow your philosophy
of letting things just be,
of listening to my heart
and simply being me.

Guru Stew 87

ELEVEN / ELEVEN

Another watch went missing eleven months ago
I didn't feel a thing when the clasp let go,
and so I bought one just the same, all shiny gold and new
but I wasn't too surprised when this went missing too.

I know my Dad's behind it, this is his little joke
a message with a symbol though not a word he spoke.
It says he's watching over me from the other side
and I should be aware of dangers that may hide.

It doesn't really matter where my gold watch went
so long as I received the message that was sent.
Advent is the time when we should watch and wait
to see what's right in front of us before it is too late.

VERY FUNNY DAD...

Dad was playing games again, he had our Mum perplexed
she couldn't find him in this row or even in the next.
Dad gave our Mum the run around looking here and there
just when she thought she'd found him he vanished in thin air.

My husband does the same to me when we go out to shop
I search for him along the aisles till I will surely drop.
He's never where I leave him, he strays and wanders off
but I can always find him by following his cough.

Dad put us off the scent that day, he made himself unseen
he made himself invisible where we had already been.
Don't let him put it over you, don't cry and make a fuss,
it isn't we who misplaced him, but he who misplaced us.

Next time we go and visit Dad we'll memorise the spot
and we'll advise him of the number of his cemetery plot.

UP THERE

They're laying up in Heaven's foyer,
Two mates from here below,
Ted and Tony on the job
Now sporting new halos.

They're rolling out red carpet
In the mansion up above.
Their wages are a job well done
And God's abiding Love.

More impressive than a Persian rug
Or the finest tapestry,
The quality of the carpet
is simply Heavenly.

They're rolling out red carpet
for the Landlord in the sky
to welcome all the guests
as Eternity goes by.

SPIRITUAL

THANK YOU

I take the pen held out to me
and all that is implied.
To hear the whispers of the soul
to write the story down
communion calling
linking thinking
reaching teaching
simple complex
words.
I take up the pen
again and again
the words are all supplied.

THE THISTLE

Through the trees the wind did whistle
and 'twas that day I saw the thistle,
in the field it was growing,
in amongst the farmers sowing.

It was purple and it was green
and it was lonely as e'er I've seen,
but then it drooped
and so I stooped
alas it died
I softly cried.

New life awaits the thistle down
as the wind tears off its thorny crown
and on the wind that whistled that day
the seed was carried far away,

Far from the field where it had grown
then back to earth the seed was sown.
From deep below I heard it cry
"The life within refused to die."

Now in its renewed state
the thistle does not hesitate,
the life within looks for the light
growing strong in God's sight.

Guru Stew 93

The roots hold fast the new creation
drawing life from its foundation.
Green sleeved limbs and purple crown
my thistle wears a glorious gown.

Mine is the thistles story
and I will claim eternal glory.

SHOAL

Palm of sensitive hand
sift softly sensual sand
soothing something unseen
awakening that which has been
distantly swept behind
barriers in the mind.

Deep beneath the surface
find a sense of purpose,
buried, concealed inside,
dug up, revealed, open wide,
lifting, sifting emotion
searching the soul saving ocean.

SAINT MARY of the CROSS MacKILLOP

From MacDonalds and MacKillops, two mighty Scottish clans
came a little baby as part of God's great plan.
The Southern Cross shone in the sky on an island way Down Under,
for here it would be seen God's grace in awe and wonder.

This babe, she was Australian, with Scottish blood and genes,
she was born to migrant parents of very meagre means.
In eighteen forty two Mary's life took hold,
blessed with Catholic parents, though sometimes poor and cold.

Home was with her family, they were always moving on,
when Mary was a child her father was long gone.
She knew first hand what others had to face, 'twas the cross she had to bear,
inspired by their poverty Mary's duty was to care.

Mary's motto was to spread the Word "by the sea and by the land",
to do what needed doing whatever the demands.
The founding of the Josephites was Mary's given role,
to feed and educate, to comfort and console.

Australian flavoured fruits the Holy Spirit gave
to nourish the whole Nation and many souls to save.
Mary's now in heaven and still she hears our call
we know her as the Saint who gave to us her "all".

Guru Stew 96

ETERNAL

Wintertime is falling
imposing frozen sleep
suspending life and sending it
into a sleep so deep.

Welcoming the rest
the trusting tree believes
that spring will follow winter
replacing long lost leaves.

The promise of new life
transforms the sleeping tree.
The vision of her life renewed
calls her to be free.

The singing of the spring
will waken her from sleep
now evermore an evergreen
her leaves and fruit will keep.

LINDA'S ISLAND

Linda's Island
where I flee to be just me,
to Be.
Linda's Island
surrounded by the sea
shaped by the sea
waves lapping shores, soaking sand
caressing, cleansing, constant, reassuring cycle
ritual of the sea.
my rock, my refuge, my strength.
Linda's Island.

TO BE STILL

It takes enormous effort to be still within a daze,
to be still and not to struggle in my medicated haze,
to be still and not to worry when my life looks like a maze,
to be still yet keep on going? This question fills my days.
To be still before my Maker's love transforming me always,
to be still and let His Healing Hand move me still to praise,
to be still and lay before you now like fallen snow ablaze.

HOLD FAST

Holding onto heaven
like stars up in the sky
this will be my motto,
my mantra, lullaby.
Holding on together
with a thread that firmly binds,
our lives are interwoven,
forever intertwined.
Holding onto signs of Love,
directing the right way
trusting in the path ahead
and never from it stray.
Holding onto promises
of Grace from God above
learning how we fit into
His everlasting Love.

DREAM STREAM

Sleep is pouring over me I'm washed along its stream
it carries my emotions to where I'll deeply dream.

Floating down the dream stream running through my mind
seeping into crevices lost memories to find.

The dream stream rises to a peak then it overflows
releasing my subconscious to tell me what it knows.

Concentration still and clear springs forth the living stream
baptism of my inner self purified in dream.

Filling up and letting go the soul pool flows on through
transforming the whole landscape, living life anew.

CALLIOPSIS

I love to see their yellow heads
waving in the grass
shouting sunshine to my soul
they cheer me as I pass.

A mass of calliopsis
worshipping the sun
my spirits raise, I'm moved to praise
transformation has begun.

The calliopsis chorus
sing a message from above
shouting sunshine to my soul
peace and joy and love.

I perceive their golden splendour
penetrate my being,
I receive the gift of
inspired inner seeing.

BE ALIVE

See the beauty of the landscape the life within your pond,
examine it in detail then rise up to see beyond.

Hear the music of the landscape play within your heart,
the rhythm, the momentum, each beat and note a part.

Touch the fabric of the landscape in the shape of you and I,
feel it in the depths where the mountains reach the sky.

Taste the flavours of the landscape savour fruit grown on the vine,
fruit that will sustain us through this life of yours and mine.

Catch the fragrance of the landscape the scent is everywhere,
the breath of life enlivens as it floats upon the air.

Know the meaning of the landscape whisper to your very soul,
secrets to be shared to make us one and whole.

ACKNOWLEDGEMENTS

The Publisher would like to acknowledge that the following poem received its first publication in The Mozzie Magazine:
FIFTYISH

The Australasian Highlander first published the following:
CLAN McLEOD
SAINT MARY of the CROSS MacKILLOP

The Wild Goose Literary e-Journal was the first place of publication for the following poems:
A SIGHT FOR SORE EYES
THAT SHED
BE ALIVE

ABOUT THE AUTHOR

Linda J McLeod has been writing and performing poetry since her adolescence. Her work has been featured in The Mozzie, The Australasian Highlander, and The Wild Goose Literary e-Journal. Linda has performed her poetry regularly at Poets in the Pub, The Katoomba Winter Magic Festival, The Blackheath Rhododendron Festival and the Blue Mountains Music Festival.

www.ingramcontent.com/pod-product-compliance
Lightning Source LLC
Chambersburg PA
CBHW032045290426
44110CB00012B/962